Machu Picchu: The History and Mystery of the Incan City

By Charles River Editors

Machu Picchu. Photo by Martin St.-Amant

About Charles River Editors

Charles River Editors was founded by Harvard and MIT alumni to provide superior editing and original writing services, with the expertise to create digital content for publishers across a vast range of subject matter. In addition to providing original digital content for third party publishers, Charles River Editors republishes civilization's greatest literary works, bringing them to a new generation via ebooks.

Sign up here to receive updates about free books as we publish them, **and visit** Our Kindle Author Page to browse today's free promotions and our most recently published Kindle titles.

Introduction

Machu Picchu with the mountain Huayna Picchu in the background. Photo by Charles J. Sharp

Machu Picchu

In 1911, American historian Hiram Bingham publicized the finding of what at the time was considered a "lost city" of the Inca. Though local inhabitants had known about it for century, Bingham documented and photographed the ruins of a 15th century settlement nestled along a mountain ridge above the Urubamba Valley in Peru, placed so perfectly from a defensive standpoint that it's believed the Spanish never conquered it and may have never known about it.

Today, of course, Machu Picchu is one of South America's best tourist spots, and the ruins have even been voted one of the Seven New Wonders of the World. But even though Machu Picchu is now the best known of all Incan ruins, its function in Incan civilization is still not clear. Some have speculated that it was an outpost or a frontier citadel, while others believe it to be a sanctuary or a work center for women. Still others suggest that it was a ceremonial center or perhaps even the last refuge of the Incas after the Spanish conquest. One of the most theories to take hold is that Machu Picchu was the summer dwelling of the Inca's royal court, the Inca's version of Versailles. As was the case with the renaming of Mayan and Aztec ruins, the names given to various structures by archaeologists are purely imaginary and thus not very helpful; for example, the mausoleum, palace or watchtower at Machu Picchu may have been nothing of the sort.

What is clear at Machu Picchu is that the urban plan and the building techniques employed followed those at other Incan settlements, particularly the capital of Cuzco. The location of plazas and the clever use of the irregularities of the land, along with the highly developed aesthetic involved in masonry work, followed the model of the Inca capital. At Machu Picchu, the typical Incan technique of meticulously assembling ashlar masonry and creating walls of blocks without a binding material is astounding. The blocks are sometimes evenly squared and sometimes are of varying shape. In the latter case, the very tight connection between the blocks of stone seems quite remarkable. Even more astounding than the precise stone cutting of the Incas is the method that they used for the transportation and movement on site of these enormous blocks. The Incas did not have the wheel, so all the work was accomplished using rollers and levers.

Machu Picchu: The History and Mystery of the Incan City comprehensively covers the history of the city, as well as the speculation surrounding the purpose of Machu Picchu and the debate over the buildings. Along with pictures and a bibliography, you will learn about Machu Picchu like you never have before, in no time at all.

Machu Picchu: The History and Mystery of the Incan City

About Charles River Editors

Introduction

    Chapter 1: The History of the Inca before the Spanish Conquest

    Chapter 2: The Logistics of Machu Picchu

    Chapter 3: Nearby Sites

    Chapter 4: Machu Picchu's Geography

    Chapter 5: Machu Picchu's Layout and Buildings

    Chapter 6: Machu Picchu in Incan History

    Chapter 7: Theories about Machu Picchu

    Chapter 8: Modern Machu Picchu

Chapter 1: The History of the Inca before the Spanish Conquest

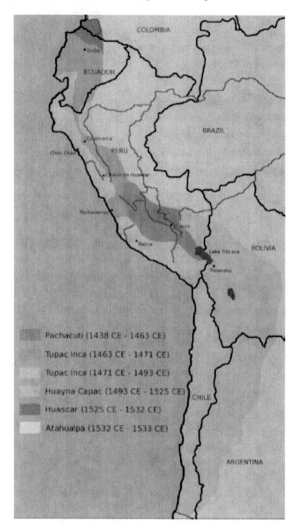

Map of the Inca Empire

According to history as created by Inca oral tradition, preserved by memory keepers and written down by Spanish commentators after the conquest, there was no culture or civilization in Peru before the Incas arrived on the scene. Given these origins, anthropologists speculate that in the interest of ensuring their dominance in the area, the Incas purposely extinguished any local histories that existed in their empire, so that for all the peoples of the empire history began when the Incas appeared. Ironically, this was accomplished in much the same way and with similar results as the Spanish attempt to destroy the Incas' own memory of their history and civilization.

The Inca people, in spite of their own propaganda or manipulated oral history, did not suddenly appear in a cultureless environment. In fact, people dwelt in the Inca lands as early as 3000 B.C., and archaeologists working at various sites have found pottery and textiles that indicate a rich history of pre-Inca Andean cultures. Among these is the Paracas culture, named by archaeologists after the Paracas Peninsula, where a rich deposit of finely woven textiles was found in shaft burials. The Paracas culture, which existed from 800-100 B.C., was based on irrigated agriculture.

Another pre-Inca culture of the region was the Moche civilization, which flourished on the coastal region of northern Peru from about 100-800 A.D. The Moche were expert builders, as the remains of their adobe temples near Huaca de la Luna testify. And around the same time the Moche were constructing their cities, the Nazca culture rose on the southern coast of Peru. It was the Nazca who etched the mysterious lines in the desert gravel around 500 A.D. that have been interpreted by conspiracy theorists and New Agers to be sophisticated Martian landing strips.

One of the most advanced pre-Inca cultures was the Tiwanaku. The remains of this culture, which was centered in northern Bolivia, indicate that it was based on sophisticated agricultural practices with terraced fields and irrigated lowlands, and that it expanded its influence through widespread conquest.

Thus, it was into this rich cultural environment that the Incas inserted their own social organization and became dominant through wars of expansion and, it is assumed, astute bureaucratic control. At Cuzco the Incas thrived under a series of rulers and under the protection of the sun god, for whom they built a temple. In the 13th century, the 8th Inca leader, Virachocha Inca, assumed the title of Sapa Inca, or unique, supreme leader. It was under his rule that the Incas began the creation of their empire by dominating the highlands around Cuzco and subjugating temporarily the Chanca people in the south of modern Peru.

In 1438, the Incas continued expanding their sphere of influence under the leadership of Pachacúti Inca Yupanqui, who after his initial conquest (or possibly re-conquest) of the Chanca placed the Inca warriors under his brother Capac Yupanqui. Unfortunately, Capac Yupanqui was unsuccessful in chasing down and slaughtering all the Chanca and was punished for his failure by forfeiting his life. It's believed that Machu Picchu, built sometime around the mid-15th century, was constructed under the orders of Pachacúti.

The next great expansion of the Inca Empire took place under Túpac Inca Yupanqui. As a prince commander, he extended the Inca Empire north into modern Ecuador, where he rebuilt the city of Quito. After ascending to the throne in about 1471, according to a Spanish commentator, he sailed out to some islands in the Pacific, which may have been the Galapagos and Easter Island, before ultimately returning to Cuzco with black slaves, gold and a chair of brass. This may be an entirely mythic voyage, but it is a fact that Túpac Inca Yupanqui was successful in pushing the frontiers of empire north into Ecuador and south into Chile.

The son of Túpac Inca Yupanqui was Huyana Capac who expanded the Inca Empire into Argentina and further into Chile. The Empire was now at its greatest extent, stretching over vast tracts of land in modern day Bolivia, Ecuador, Columbia, Peru, Chile and Argentina. It is thought that Huyana Capac died of smallpox, which by now was spreading rapidly from Spanish dominated Central America. It was Huyana Capac's two sons, Húascar and Atahualpa, who became engaged in civil war just prior to the arrival of the Spanish.

Chapter 2: The Logistics of Machu Picchu

Machu Picchu is a breathtaking sight, and when viewing the site, it's easy to overlook all the details, but just about everyone who sees it stops at one point to wonder just how the Inca accomplished what they did. Even with modern highways, Machu Picchu is hardly the easiest place to reach, and that doesn't even take into account how the Inca built the city once they got the necessary materials to the spot.

The Incan empire - also known by its Quechua name "Tawantinsuyu" - was divided into four unequally-sized quadrants called "suyu", with the capital of Cuzco at the center. The northwestern (Chinchay Suyu) and southeastern (Qulla Suyu) were vast areas that stretched along the spine of the Andes, but, the region that Machu Picchu inhabits is in the northeastern suyu, the Anti Suyu.[1] Anti Suyu was one of the heartlands of the Empire, as it included the valley of Urubamba and other key areas. In the highly stratified environment of the Incan Empire, the nobility of Anti Suyu was the third highest rung of the society, just below the Emperor and his family and the non-royal elites of Cuzco itself[2].

Some knowledge about the social structures of the Incan Empire is necessary to understand where scholars think Machu Picchu fit within the larger picture. At the bedrock of Incan society was an institution called the "ayllu", which was a series of inter-related families that made up a single community and operated as the local government and economy. Generally speaking, ayllu were able to produce all that they needed for everyday consumption, while turning to the wider empire as a whole in times of disaster. The ayllu primarily provided labor in the form of military conscripts to the empire at large.[3]

The Inca, like other indigenous groups in Central America and South America, liked to claim they were the original inhabitants of the region, but in actuality they were not even the first to weld the ayllu into a wider political polity. An elite had existed in the Andes for centuries, and they had created numerous powerful states. While none of them came even close to the Inca in size, power or architectural glory, they did lay the social foundations that the Inca built upon. These were not egalitarian hunting societies or small farming groups, but highly stratified societies where the vast majority of the populace fulfilled the roles they were born into. There was no merchant class, and what

---

1 *La Cultura Incaica* (1965) by Hans Horkheimer and Frederico Kauffman. Lima. Pg 23.
2 Horkheimer and Kauffman (1965), pg 62, 80.
3 "The Inca Model of Statecraft" by Michael Mosley from *The Incas and Their Ancestors* (1992), Thames and Hudson Publishing pp 49-53. Accessed online at:
http://web.mesacc.edu/dept/d10/asb/anthro2003/archy/aymara/inca_model.html

existed of a "middle" class was made up of government administrators beholden to the elites. It was this centralized, state-directed economic system that has led some scholars to describe the Inca as a "socialist" empire.[4]

What does all this mean for Machu Picchu? Despite its isolation on a mountain peak, any project of such magnitude had to be a product of the most powerful social forces of Incan society. In the case of Machu Picchu, these forces were the absolute monarchy based in Andean tradition but forged into an unprecedented world power by the great Inca ruler Pachacúti, as well as the systems of labor tribute that brought thousands of workers to the lofty summits of mounts Machu Picchu and Huayna Picchu in the mid-1400s.

Unfortunately, Machu Picchu is a product of a society that did not leave written records, and on top of that, the Inca experienced massive social upheaval and destruction at the hands of the Spanish only decades after Machu Picchu was being built. This means that some of the most crucial details about the builders of the site - where they came from, how many there were, and so on - are forever lost. There are numerous estimates as to how many people worked on the site and for how long, but what is known is that the project took thousands of laborers decades to construct, and it must have placed a considerable strain on even the great empire's funds.

The laborers were probably not enslaved peoples as modern society thinks of slaves, meaning they were probably not owned as property by the Incan emperor, and they probably were not a special category considered to be sub-human. Instead, the project was probably built in the manner of all great Incan public works, including the empire's famous roads and major fortifications: the mit'a. In addition to providing military conscripts, the ayllu also provided mit'a, which was a social construct that utilized the people of the empire for public labor. Just like in Ancient Egypt, farmers and laborers in the Incan Empire did not pay their taxes in currency or food but instead in labor. After they finished their time on their own farms, they would owe the state a debt of labor for a number of days and thus be sent to a public project, where they would spend a set number of weeks laboring for the public good. Of course, the public good was often loosely defined, since the work was often for the personal profit or pleasure of the Incan elite (as many suspect was the case for Machu Picchu itself). During this time, the laborers' families would be fed and provisioned out of the public storehouses.[5]

This constant and massive source of labor ensured that the Empire always had workers on hand for huge projects, and it also meant that it is very difficult for scholars today to estimate a "cost" of the project. These workers would have been laboring on some public project whether Machu Picchu was built or not, and the majority of the materials in the citadel were gathered on-site and thus not purchased. Hence, the project was not a drain directly on the coffers of the state but instead in the form of workers diverted from other potential projects. If there was a "debt" accrued by the creation of Machu Picchu, it was in the form of agricultural yields not boosted by extra irrigation, areas that were less safe by the lack of protective fortresses, or communities not linked to the empire because of delays

---

4 *El Imperio Socialista de los Incas 7 Edicion* (1972) by Louis Baudin. Jose Antonion Arze (trans.). Santiago, Chile: Ediciones Rodas S.A.

5 "Mit'a." (2005). In *Iberia and the Americas: Culture, Politics, and History*. Retrieved from http://www.credoreference.com.libezproxy2.syr.edu/entry/abcibamrle/mit'a

in road-building. At the same time, the fact that the Empire in this era was constantly expanding meant that the pool of labor was constantly growing, so the diversion of some of these laborers (which may have even numbered in the tens of thousands) to Machu Picchu was probably not felt directly as a loss if there were still more laborers coming in from conquered lands all the time.

This type of economics is quite different from the way modern societies tend to think about public works projects today, but it was not unusual in the ancient world or the Middle Ages. Many empires had permanently instituted mass labor. For example, the Roman legions, when not fighting, would be constantly working on public projects like fortifications (including Hadrian's Wall in the north of England). Other empires used prisoners of war or criminals, such as the work teams that constructed the Great Wall of China, and a system similar to that of the Incan mit'a was instituted in Ancient Egypt to make use of farmers during the flood season when they could not work their fields. This practice, often called "corvée" labor, continued well into the 19th and 20th centuries, including road crews in the American South, as well as public works projects in nations like Russia, Haiti and Japan.

However, as the empire continued to age and expand, the mit'a work teams were not as easily diverted to projects like Machu Picchu, which may be one of the reasons the building feat was never matched by later generations. In later years, the new conquests were in locations increasingly distant from the center of Cuzco, making it difficult to bring in fresh laborers during the allotted mit'a period. Also, the Empire had an increasing burden of maintenance on their extensive network of roads, irrigation systems, fortifications and public structures, all of which required the diversion of large numbers of laborers on a constant basis. To divert workers from these projects in the latter stages of the empire would have undermined the infrastructure that allowed the empire to function as it currently existed. Diverting workers from a potential project had far fewer short-term consequences than diverting laborers from the maintenance of an existing public work.

While Machu Picchu is considered the Inca's masterpiece, the success of Inca architecture was a byproduct of their ability to assimilate the work and techniques of past cultures. The exacting masonry of Inca municipal buildings, paved roads, bridges, irrigation canals and agricultural terraces was not unprecedented in the region. The Incas assimilated and developed techniques of art and architecture that were already practiced in the cultures that they conquered and incorporated into their Empire.

During Pachacúti's expansionist conquests, the Inca defeated the people of Tiwanaku in western Bolivia around 1450, right around the time construction was beginning on Machu Picchu. The city the Inca vanquished was a substantial one in which the buildings were constructed of precisely cut stone, smoothly polished and assembled in interlocking courses or layers. Tiwanaku was not a minor country outpost; archaeologists and historians speculate it may have had upwards of 285,000-1,500,000 inhabitants and controlled a large empire that it had apparently acquired over several centuries.

Pachacúti was certainly impressed by the substantial glory of Tiwanaku, and as part of the tribute mit'a, he took masons to Cuzco and set them to work transforming the inferior adobe village into a highly organized symbol of power, constructed with stone. The rebuilt Cuzco was planned on the shape of a puma, which was inserted between the two rivers Huatanay and Tullumayo. Canals were then built with masonry walls to protect the city from flooding. A grid plan with narrow streets was established and plazas were laid out, with the city's blocks lined with kancha or compounds of buildings surrounded by masonry walls. The city at its greatest extent housed more than 40,000 inhabitants, and with suburban settlements was estimated by a commentator in 1553 to have had a population of 200,000.

Gate of the Sun at Tiwanaku (modern day Bolivia)

The administration of the Inca Empire was such that the forms of buildings and town planning established at Cuzco in the 1450's was repeated in a standardized form in building campaigns elsewhere up until the Spanish conquest. This was not unlike the municipal building programs that the British would establish through their empire. The idea that Cuzco was the center of an Empire that was comprised of four provinces was manifest in the planning of the city, where there was a central intersection of the four roads that led to the four divisions of the Empire.

Archaeologists have studied a number of cities and towns built by the Inca's in various reaches of the Empire. In the Peruvian town of Ollantaytambo, the Incas repeated their grid plan in organizing the urban architecture, even though it stretches over uneven ground. They also repeated the form of building that was developed at Cuzco, with large and small rectangular spaces of a single story roofed with thatch supported on a wooden framework. This town, unfinished at the time of the Spanish conquest, was linked to Machu Picchu by a stone paved road. On a steep mountainside adjacent to the city there are remains of several houses or grain storage chambers clustered together. The rectangular rooms would have been covered by thatched roofs supported on a ridge pole running between the stone gabled ends.

Granaries or houses on hillside at Ollantaytambo

What is clear at Machu Picchu is that the urban plan and the building techniques employed followed those at Cuzco. The location of plazas and the clever use of the irregularities in the land, along with the highly developed aesthetic involved in masonry work, follow the model of the Inca capital. The typical Incan technique of meticulously assembling ashlar masonry and creating walls of blocks without a binding material is astounding. The blocks are sometimes evenly squared and sometimes are of varying shape. In the latter case, the very tight connection between the blocks of stone seems quite remarkable. Even more astounding than the precise stone cutting of the Inca is the method that they used for the transportation and movement of these enormous blocks. The Inca did not have the wheel, so all the work was accomplished using rollers and levers.

The Inca did not develop a way of creating vaults of stone, so all of their structures are thus based on simple two-dimensional geometry. Because the architectural repertoire of the Incas did not include the arch or the vault, their buildings are all one story in height, the doorways and windows are headed by flat stones and are thus limited in breadth, and the ceilings are the underside of the thatched roofs.

Chapter 3: Nearby Sites

As is fitting for a region of such prestige yet outside the capital city itself, Anti Suyu was also home to a number of other palaces. By examining these palaces, which were built by the same society for many of the same reasons (though at different times), it becomes possible to understand both how Machu Picchu is unique and also how it is an exemplar of a family of similar places. The Incan elites seemed to have had a fondness for mountain-top sanctuaries, and the Machu Picchu region is home to relatively large number of palaces, including the ruins of Llactapata, Choquequirao, and Vitcos. All of these sites were connected to Cuzco via the Anti Suyu branch of the famous Incan road network.

A good place to start making comparison with other palaces is at the neighboring site of Llactapata ("High Town"), which is located within visual distance of Machu Picchu itself. In fact, people now go to Llactapata partly because it offers some great views of the more famous site across the Urubamba

River valley.[6] Llactapata's location had been known for some time - Bingham noted it during his search for Machu Picchu - but it was only in 2003 that the full extent of the site was uncovered using infrared aerial photography. As it turned out, Llactapata was far more extensive than originally believed, and it seemed to be linked to its sister site across the river. In addition to apparently serving as a storage and distribution center for Machu Picchu, Llactapata's central sun temple and other structures were directly aligned with those in the larger site of Machu Picchu as well.[7] Whether that was intentional or not is still unclear, because these alignments may have been due to the fact that the two nearby sites were both simultaneously directing their attention to the same surrounding geographical features. This means that as more becomes known about Llactapata's layout, it might be possible to determine how Machu Picchu was aligned to the landscape itself.[8]

Further along the ancient roads lie the ruins of Choquequirao.[9] Sometimes called "the other Machu Picchu," Choquequirao is built in a similar style, seemingly as a fortress city with palaces and temples built around a central plaza. Choquequirao was built at a later date than Machu Picchu, during the reigns of Tupac Inca Yupanqui (1471-1493) and Huayna Capac (1493-1527), the son and grandson of Pachacúti respectively. The facility had extensive terraces, like at Machu Picchu, and it was aligned with the sun and surrounding landscapes. While it is impossible to know for certain, it is probable that Tupac Inca and Huayna Capac had Machu Picchu in mind when they ordered the site's construction, but the differences in geography and the lack of easily accessible monumental stones meant that the architecture in Choquequirao never lived up to the grandeur of its predecessor.

---

6 "Machu Picchu's Observatory the Re-Discovery of Llactapata and its Sun-Temple" by J. McKim Malville, accessed online at http://www.bibliotecapleyades.net/arqueologia/esp_machu_picchu08.htm
7 "Explorers Reveal Riches of Machu Picchu's Neglected Neighbor" by John Noble Wilford in the *New York Times* 18 Nov 2003.
8 "Scientists find Machu Picchu 'lost' suburb: Fourth Edition" by Thomas H. Maugh II in the *Seattle Times* 9 Nov 2003, p. A.11
9 "The Other Machu Picchu" by Ethan Todras-Whitehill, published in the *New York Times*, 3 June 2007. Accessed online at http://www.nytimes.com/2007/06/03/travel/03inca.html?pagewanted=all&_r=0

Choquequirao

Ruins at Choquequirao. Photo by Harley Calvert

Choquequirao appears to have been built by prisoners imported from the Chachapoya people of northern Peru, who were conquered by the two Inca leaders. Scholars believe this because their architectural fingerprints can be seen in the structures. Choquequirao guarded the entrance to a region of Peru known as Vilcamba, which was the last stronghold of the Incas in the colonial period, and the Inca somehow kept Choquequirao a secret from the Spanish. Choquequirao was never attacked or looted, and it maintained regular contact and movement of people back and forth from Cuzco[10].

Vitcos is located the furthest of the four from Cuzco and is believed to be the last holdout of the highest Incan elite after the Spanish invasion.[11] The exact date of the site's construction is disputed, with arguments that it was another project of Pachacúti's or that it was constructed for the rebellious Inca, Manco Inca, father of the final famous leader, Túpac Amaru. Vitcos is much smaller than the other sites mentioned here, serving more as an echo of remembered grandeur. However, it still had some of the elements of its predecessors: a central plaza, stone buildings and a dramatic location on a high point.

What do these sites say about Machu Picchu? First, the sites allow for an understanding about the

---

10 "Choquequirao, Topa Inca's Machu Picchu: a royal estate and ceremonial center" by Gary R. Ziegler and J. McKim Malville, published in the *Proceedings of the International Astronomical Union International Symposium on Archaeoastronomy* Jan 2011: 162-168

11 "In the Shadow of Machu Picchu" (2011) by Andrea Minarcek, published in *Arthur Frommer's* (July/August 2011: 15-16), accessed online at http://search.proquest.com.libezproxy2.syr.edu/docview/876966164

distinctiveness of Machu Picchu. To some extent, Machu Picchu's fame has steadily built upon itself, ensuring that it remains a heavily toured site simply because of its reputation. But at the same time, it's clear that the Inca considered Machu Picchu to be a place of remarkable beauty and importance. Later complexes echoed its design but were unable to emulate its scope and grandeur. Even in the twilight of their civilization, the last Inca constructed a smaller version of Machu Picchu as their final stronghold.

Chapter 4: Machu Picchu's Geography

While the buildings of Machu Picchu would be undoubtedly impressive anywhere, the fact that they are located on a high ridgeline over a verdant tropical valley make them all the more awe-inspiring. The selection of this site was probably due at least in part to the self-confidence amongst Cuzco elites after a series of spectacular conquests, but it is also due to a deep relationship between the Inca and the land itself. Machu Picchu not only sits within the landscape; it is fundamentally a product of it. This is a major difference between Machu Picchu and similar kinds of sites in the European world, which mostly ignored the peculiarities of local topography and instead built upon a universalized model that was transported from one point of the world to another. This can be seen in places as diverse as the perfect geometrical gardens of European palaces to the numbered, rectilinear grids of North American cities like Salt Lake City, New York City and Bogotá.

The Incan elite saw themselves as rulers of the known world, but in their worldview, their empire could not be divorced from its location. It was a power tied to the central city of Cuzco, to the spirits of the mountains, and to the landscape in general. Hence, understanding the structures at Machu Picchu requires understanding the landscape surrounding it and on which it was built. The builders of the site appeared not to have viewed the landscape as a challenge to overcome but as a fundamental part of the structure of the complex they were planning.

Machu Picchu overlooks the Urubamba River, which is one of the many headwaters of the mighty Amazon River. The Urubamba River begins to the southeast of Cuzco, near the southern boundaries of today's Peru, and it flows northwest and eventually joins the Apurímac River, where the two rivers form the Ucayali River. The Ucayali River finally joins the Amazon in northern Peru and then turns east on an inexorable march to the sea. Traditionally, the Urubamba has been divided by Hispano-Peruvians into two sections: the Upper and Lower. The Upper River is the section that passes under Machu Picchu, as well as through some classic Incan lands, many of which are still densely populated and irrigated today. After an infamous canyon whitewater called the Pongo de Mainique, it becomes the Lower River, which enters the less-populated rainforests of northeastern Peru[12].

As the Upper Urubamba passes northwards (but long before the rapids of the Pongo), it enters an area known as the "Sacred Valley of the Inca." This region was one of the heartlands of the Incan power, it was densely populated, and today it is rich with ruins of that time and before. Part of its value came from the fact that the local climate facilitated the growth of corn (maize), a crop that was often difficult to produce in the cold highlands but which was a valuable staple of the Incan diet. As the frontiers of

---

12 "Urubamba." (2013). In *The Columbia Encyclopedia*. Retrieved from http://www.credoreference.com.libezproxy2.syr.edu/entry/columency/urubamba

Pachacúti's ever-growing empire pressed further and further from the center of Cuzco, the Sacred Valley became an increasingly secure breadbasket close to the capital. This had a heavy influence on where Machu Picchu was located, and it was the reason the location could support a spectacular palace befitting the Incan emperor. Similar processes were at work in the selection of the locations for other "summer" palaces around the world, such as Versailles on the outskirts of Paris or even the modern Camp David presidential retreat in the United States.

The Royal Palace at Machu Picchu

Machu Picchu's renown comes not only from its size and beauty but also from its dramatic location perched on a high saddle overlooking the Urubamba Valley. Machu Picchu is located 7,710 feet above sea level in a saddle between two peaks: Mt. Machu Picchu (6,530 feet) and Huayna Picchu (8,858 feet). Machu Picchu is located on the upward slope of the Huayna Picchu side, so it is actually located higher than the mountain it is named after.[13] In contrast, the capital city of Cuzco is located at 11,200 feet above sea level, but because of Machu Picchu's placement on a ridgeline, Cuzco is only slightly cooler than Machu Picchu. Year round, Cuzco has an average high of 67.5° F and an average low of 40° F, while Machu Picchu has averages of 69.4° and 42.8° F.[14] In the surrounding valleys, however, the climate is much warmer, as evidenced by the lush rainforests that the Machu Picchu vista is so famous for.

The mountains themselves were integrated into the complex in other ways as well. The famous Incan

---

13 "Machu Picchu: Supplemental Information" at the *Encyclopedia Britannica*, accessed online at: http://global.britannica.com/EBchecked/topic/354719/Machu-Picchu/354719suppinfo/Supplemental-Information
14 Weather Data From The World Weather Information Service (http://worldweather.wmo.int/029/c00110.htm), BBC Weather (http://www.bbc.co.uk/weather/3941584) and World Weather Online (http://www.worldweatheronline.com/v2/weather-averages.aspx?q=MFT)

highways connecting the site to Cuzco trace their way up the peaks' sides, and there are numerous smaller buildings. One of the most famous of these buildings is the Temple of the Moon, a name chosen by Bingham more for its poetry than any evidence that it had anything to do with the moon. The Temple was a relatively shallow cave in the side of Huayna Picchu which was expanded and heavily modified by the builders. The focus of this cavern is a stone throne which stands before stairs to a deeper room. It is believed that the throne once held a sacred mummy, a relatively common phenomenon amongst the Inca.15

The Temple of the Moon

The Machu Picchu complex is not only located within this landscape but fundamentally shaped by it. One of the easiest manifestations of this can be seen by the untrained eye and was noted by the earliest archaeologists: the maintenance of natural outcroppings. The construction of the site required a major effort at building uneven surfaces and removing troublesome rocks to create flat building surfaces. This is not surprising, since any building project on uneven terrain has to find ways to create level planes for the construction of floors and roofs. What is surprising, however, is the number of natural outcroppings that the Inca left in place. The Inca believed that they were descended from the earth goddess Pachamama, and that their society and their blood were only made possible by the blessings and infusions of her essence into them. In Machu Picchu and other Incan structures, this was practically manifested by the melding of stone outcroppings and buildings. As Carolyn Dean explains, "By providing firm, petrous foundations for Inka structures, ... Pachamama... appears to have readily consented to, if not actually joined in, Inka building activity. Because integrated outcrops occupy the

---

15 "The Temple of the Moon and Huayna Picchu" in the Moon Guide, accessed online at:
http://www.moon.com/destinations/peru/machu-picchu/machu-picchu-hikes-and-treks/temple-the-moon-and-huayna-picchu

interface between nature and art, they exist simultaneously as parts of, and blur the boundary dividing, natural and built environments."16 At Machu Picchu, it was not only outcroppings but also caverns which were absorbed into the layout, as with the Temple of the Moon on Huayna Picchu.

On a grander scale, the layout of Machu Picchu conforms not only to the landscape of the saddle between the peaks but also the positions of the surrounding mountains themselves. Throughout the site, doors and windows are placed to capture particular views of the mountains, and occasionally the buildings were accompanied by natural outcroppings reshaped to mimic the distant mountain.17

At the same time, the natural landscape was not the only thing the builders incorporated into the site. While the Spanish eventually destroyed most of the Incan holy sites, archaeologists have determined that amongst the surviving wreckage, there are distinctive alignments between celestial phenomena and the sacred buildings. This is particularly true of the sun; the Inca placed the worship of the sun at the center of their religious life and viewed the royal family as descendants of the solar deities. Their sacred calendar was built around the solar cycles, and it should come as no surprise that sites at and beyond Machu Picchu have shown connections to important events, such as eclipses.18

Many of Machu Picchu's alignments have become apparent only after the recent excavations of Llactapata, its smaller sister site. When lines are drawn between significant elements of the two sites, several of them are found to correspond to the equinox and the June solstice. The most important solstice line runs through Machu Picchu's Sacred Plaza, the Intihuatana in the valley town of Pisac, and the Sun Temple of Llactapata. The other solstice line connects the Three Window's house on the side of Huayna Picchu with the Overlook Temple in Llactapata. One of the equinox lines connects Llactapata's Overlook Temple to the summit of Mount Machu Picchu, and the other connects a stone platform at the north end of Llactapata and the summit of the nearby peak of Cerro San Miguel, which lies between Llactapata and Machu Picchu. Within Machu Picchu itself, the June equinox lines appear again and again. They govern the alignments of walls in the palace, an opening in one of the smaller temples, the overlook in the Central Plaza, the placement and shape of the Intihuatana stone, and the directions of several minor pathways and buildings.19

Given the manner in which the landscape and Machu Picchu are inseparable, it is perhaps fortuitous that Bingham named his great "discovery" after the mountain it was found on.

Chapter 5: Machu Picchu's Layout and Buildings

Machu Picchu is divided into two roughly equivalent sections. To the south, there are a series of elaborate cultivation terraces, and to the north is the "urban" sector, which contained the primary

---

16 "The Inka Married the Earth: Integrated Outcrops and the Making of Place" by Carolyn Dean, in *The Art Bulletin* (Sept 2007): 89, 3. p 502
17 "Machu Picchu, Inca Pachacuti's Sacred City: A Multiple Ritual, Ceremonial and Administrative Center" (2003) by Gary Ziegler and J. McKim Malville. Accessed online at:
http://inkaterra.com/media/pdf/pdf_machu_picchu_pueblo_hotel/mpinthepress/MPIncaPachacutiSacredCity.pdf
18 *Archaeoastronomical survey of Inca sites in Peru* by Zawaski, Mike J. Masters Thesis. University of Northern Colorado, ProQuest, UMI Dissertations Publishing, 2007. 1445097.
19 Ziegler and McKim Malville. (2003)

buildings of the complex. The urban sector is higher in elevation, as it located closer to the summit of Huayna Picchu. Dividing the two sectors is a stone wall which originally had a single small gate on its western edge (though modern visitors enter the complex closer to the center). Overall, the complex has over 200 rooms, and at first blush, the layout seems strange to Westerners because the walls are often not straight and the corners are not square. However, the careful fit of the stones indicates that they were definitely designed like this, and the laborers often took advantage of natural curves in the underlying terrain. And while Machu Picchu may not have been designed specifically as a fortress, as a home of the Incan emperor himself, it was certainly well-guarded.

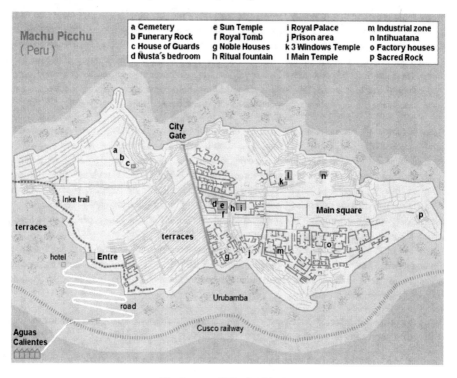

The layout of Machu Picchu

The terraces at Machu Picchu

The residential section of the urban sector. Photo by Christophe Meneboeuf.

The buildings of the various parts of the urban sector form discrete named groups separated by alleys. The temples and shrines in the facility were used for ancestor worship and when Bingham arrived, one of the categories of objects he looted from the site were ancestral mummies which were kept in these shrines.

The urban sector is built around a central plaza. Directly to the south of the Plaza and located in the center of the complex near the edge of terraces is the Royal Palace, as well as the Royal Tomb, the round Temple of the Sun and the Ritual Fountains. To the east of this plaza is an elaborate collection of buildings called the Houses of Factory Workers and the Industrial Zone. To the west are the Main Temple, the House of the High Priest, the Temple of Three Windows and the Intihuatana (the famous "Hitching Post of the Sun"). Finally, to the north, residents would have to climb up to the Sacred Rock and then continue out of the complex to the Temple of the Moon. Thus, it's possible to understand how the urban sector was divided from the Central Plaza: to the south were the royal dwellings, to the east the homes and workshops of the workers, to the west the sacred area inhabited by priests, and to the north the Sacred Rock.[20]

The Temple of the Sun

There were a few specialized sections as well, including a prison and the Temple of the Condor

---

[20] *Machu Picchu, Antologia* (1963) by H. Buse, published Comision Nacional de Cultura del Peru. Lima, Peru.

between the industrial area and the palace and a rock quarry in the western zone. A large aqueduct brought water from the central spring (the "Ritual Fountains") in the Palace to the rest of the facility.

It's important to keep in mind that the names of the buildings are not the original ones, which have been lost to history, so all of them are based on guesswork. Some names, like the Royal Palace, are probably pretty good indications of the buildings' original uses, while others are simply descriptive, like the Temple of Three Windows and the Intihuatana. The fact that the buildings are formed in groups helps with the naming process, as does the ability to identify temples from the presence of mummies and other architectural elements.

Temple of the Three Windows

The Royal Palace is probably the most important structure in the complex, especially if the dominant interpretation of the site's purpose as a royal retreat is true. The Royal Palace is the largest building and is centrally located on the Central Plaza, and it is also between the agricultural terraces and the urban sector, ensuring that it would have been conspicuously visible to anyone approaching Machu Picchu from the Incan road. The building was the first place where water entered the site after being gathered from a spring high on Huayna Picchu and sent by aqueduct, meaning the people inhabiting the palace received the cleanest water.

The palace was prominently located for the rest of Machu Picchu's inhabitants to see, but it also afforded spectacular views itself. The palace looked out onto the Central Plaza, and some of its walls were aligned with the rising and setting sun on the June equinox. Besides its grandeur and placement, one of the pieces of evidence that shows that it was a place of particular importance is the existence of numerous "double jamb" doors. Incan doors were constructed in a trapezoidal pattern, and double jambs had an inner lip several centimeters deep around the edge of the door that may have held a special ceremonial door or another divider that separated the elite quarters from the eyes and presence of the non-elites. The Palace's use of these doors shows that it was intended for the use of the highest members of Incan society.[21]

An Incan Double Jamb Doorway

---

[21] "Palacio" in Buse 1963 pp 65; "Inca Architecture: Less is More-- Much More!" accessed online at http://www.rutahsa.com/incaarch.html

This building at Machu Picchu has trapezoidal windows. Photo by Martin St-Amant.

One of the more enigmatic and interesting constructs in the complex is the stone monolith that Bingham named the "Intihuatana," a Quechua term he coined that roughly translates to "Hitching Post of the Sun." It takes the form of an upright stone set on a large shaped base, and the entire construct stands on top of an elevated platform made of several terraces. The stone's many sides are masterfully carved to both mimic the form of Mount Machu Picchu in the distance but also to track the movements of the sun in regards to Solstices and Equinoxes. At one time, these stone sculptures were found throughout Incan territory and were central to the empire's official sun cult, but the Spanish destroyed almost all of them, so the Intihuatana of Machu Picchu is that much more invaluable as an archaeological remain. Also important is the fact that this Intihuatana is similar to one that still remains in the village of Písac in the valley below, as well as the fact that the two are aligned with each other, creating an even-more complex celestial system.[22]

---

22 "Intihuatana" in Buse 1963 pp 74.

The Intihuatana at Machu Picchu, which likely served as a solar calendar. It points directly at the Sun during the Winter Solstice. Photo by Jordan Klein.

The primary ceremonial center of complex was the Central Plaza, but for the elites of the period, the most important rituals probably occurred in the Temple of the Sun. Also protected by double jamb doors, this facility was integrated into the natural rock outcroppings of the mountain and had windows through which the sun could be tracked. In addition to being a place for rituals, it probably served as an observatory as well, and it's possible the Inca did not differentiate between the two functions.[23]

As noted earlier, the Inca assimilated the building techniques of other cultures, but the date of Machu Picchu's construction ensured that it was built during the golden days of the empire and thus used the finest techniques, designs and materials available before Pizarro and his conquistadores arrived. This is unlike other important sites, such as Cuzco, which was inhabited long before the empire's ascent and continues to be a major city today, and Tiwanaku, another major archaeological site eclipsed by the rise of the Inca.

At the heart of Machu Picchu's architecture is a mastery of granite. The builders of Machu Picchu were masters of construction from the bottom up, and recent archeology has shown that underneath the elaborate terraces, the builders created layers of waste granite, gravel, and topsoil to drain the

---

[23] "The Temple of the Sun" in the Machu Picchu Gateway, accessed online at http://www.machupicchu.org/ruins/the_temple_of_the_sun.htm

construction site. The terraces constructed in this way around the edge of the complex served to assist in the drainage higher up, thereby providing the entire complex with a remarkable level of stability and allowing it to remain preserved where it sat, perched high upon the ridgeline.

Water engineering was a central feature of Machu Picchu as well. Water was collected from a natural spring high on Huayna Picchu and then sent to the central palace, where it then drains downwards both in geography and social ranking. The site has 16 fountains, all of which drain 25 gallons a minute. The water begins at the Royal Palace and moves downhill through all of the other fountains, providing not only a system of drinking water but also an elaborate sewage system. The fact that the complex was designed and constructed as a single unit means that the hydraulic network functions – even today – with elegant, gravity-powered simplicity[24].

When the original builders arrived at the site, they encountered one of the most unsuitable landscapes for building a massive complex of buildings imaginable. However, they ended up developing an ingenious system of layered foundations which eventually created the level surfaces visible in the urban sector today. One archaeological analysis has estimated that 60% of the labor that went into building Machu Picchu was invested in the basements and foundations alone[25].

Moving up from the foundations and drainage, the next indicator of Incan brilliance comes from the granite walls themselves. The walls of Machu Picchu are famously built of stones laid without mortar, and the stones fit so tightly that it is still not possible to fit a knife blade between some of them, despite five centuries of wear, tear and disuse. The distinctive white granite of Machu Picchu makes a striking contrast to the lush green of the surrounding landscape, and the construction of the walls is even more impressive when considering that the Inca did not have metal tools. The stones were cut using wedges and hammers, then carefully shaped using grinding stones and sand. The complex also has features cut out of the living granite of the mountains, most notably the stairways and foundations. The fusion of building materials and the actual land makes the entire complex seem as though it literally grew out of the landscape on which it is situated.

---

24 "A Marvel of Inca Engineering" At NOVA, 1 Jan 2010, accessed online on
   http://www.pbs.org/wgbh/nova/ancient/wright-inca-engineering.html
25 *The Machu Picchu Guidebook* (2001) by R.M. Wright and A. Valencia Zagarra. Boulder: Johnson Books.

Inca masonry. Photo by Hakan Svensson.

The Incan builders created their stone walls to last. The walls were wider at the base than at the top, with outer faces that tapered up, meaning the stones on the lower courses are larger and the stones gradually get smaller as they worked their way upwards. In some of the finest examples, massive single-stone lintels were used over doorways to maintain stability. This style resists the forces of freezing and thawing that otherwise ruin stone walls, a basic principle used in dry stone wall construction around the globe.[26] However, the Inca took these principles to a level of perfection rarely seen elsewhere: clean fitting stones set together to create a smooth and unbroken surface centuries later. These walls were allowed to show their natural beauty because plaster was never applied to their surface.[27]

Like other forms of art among the cultures in the Andes, Incan architecture was based around the principles of symmetry. Symmetrical pottery, buildings, jewelry, and textiles were all typical of the region, and earlier Andean cultures had perfected the techniques of stone work and developed the architectural knowledge of how to manipulate the forms of buildings to control the experience of visitors. Tiwanaku, the site whose architecture was mimicked by the Inca at Cuzco, was so well known for its dramatic stonework that it was a site of pilgrimage for residents in the region.[28]

---

[26] "Dry Stone Walling: A Guide to Good Practice" accessed online at
http://www.stoneandgardens.co.uk/guidetogoodpractice.html
[27] *La Ciudad Perdida de Incas (The Lost City of the Incas)* by Hiram Bingham 1950, pg 21-23
[28] *Art of the Andes: From Chavín to Inca* (2012) by Rebecca Stone, Thames and Hudson Ltd

Chapter 6: Machu Picchu in Incan History

The Incan Empire was a relatively recent development in highland South America when Francisco Pizarro Gonzáles (c. 1471-1541) and the Spanish arrived. Highly organized hierarchical societies with advanced technologies and large cities had existed in the Andes for centuries, but it was only after the ascension of Pachacúti to the throne of the relatively small Kingdom of Cuzco that the many disparate kingdoms began to consolidate into what became the Incan Empire. Machu Picchu was literally the embodiment of Pachacúti's incredible reign, and it was only made possible by the empire's concentration of wealth and power through conquest.

Pachacúti was born in roughly 1400 in Cuzco, the child of the Sapa Inca (a term that means "Great Inca," or roughly "Great King") Huiracocha Inca and his wife Mama Runto. Huiracocha Inca was the eighth ruler of his line in Cuzco and descended from the Hanan dynasty, which came to power in Cuzco in 1350 with the reign of Inca Roca, Pachacúti's great-grandfather.

Royal transition in this period was somewhat tenuous. Huiracocha came to power after the assassination of his predecessor and his predecessor's sons, and after his own death, his preferred son Urco came to the throne. Huiracocha had attempted to guarantee succession by having a period of co-governance with Urco, but Urco was infamous for his "perversions," alcoholism and cowardice on the field of battle. At the same time, his younger brother, Pachacúti, was a rising star amongst the people of Cuzco, especially after winning several battles. Urco and Huiracocha plotted Pachacúti murder, but he managed to thwart the plan and captured and killed his brother, having his bodied quartered.

With the rival claimant removed, Pachacúti ascended to the throne of Cuzco in 1438 and ruled until roughly 1471-72. 33-34 years is a long reign for a king under any circumstance, and this extensive period gave Pachacúti the chance to realize his incredible imperial dreams. His early rivals were the Chanca people, whose invasion he thwarted near the end of his father's reign and who plagued the reign of his brother. After defeating the Chancas, Pachacúti went on parallel campaigns of conquest and re-organization. His armies thundered up and down the Andes, bringing an unprecedented number of kingdoms to heel, and back at home he established the mit'a, massively renovated Cuzco, reformed the educational system, reorganized the agriculture and built palaces and citadels, the mightiest of which is believed to be Machu Picchu.[29]

Tales of a great golden city somewhere to the south in the Andes spurred Pizarro to attempt to reach this lustrous goal. It was only on his third attempt to discover the fabled riches of the Inca Empire that Pizarro achieved his goal, and as it is said, history would never be the same.

---

29 "The Life of Pachacuti Inca Yupangui" http://www.accessmylibrary.com/article-1G1-141997158/life-pachacuti-inca-yupangui.html

Pizarro

In 1532 Pizarro marched south from Panama into Inca territory with a force that consisted of 168 men, 1 cannon and 27 horses. As he progressed, he recruited disaffected indigenous people who were apparently happy to join an expedition against their Inca overlords.

Pizarro's army first engaged in battle with the Andean natives who were subjects of the Incas on the island of Puná (near Guayaquil, Equador). He handily routed them and established a garrison at there. While engaged in solidifying his position, Pizarro's cohort, Hernando de Soto, returned from an expedition into the interior and reported that the King of the Inca, Atahualpa, wished to meet Pizarro. A consummate opportunist, like all successful conquistadors, Pizarro, not waiting for reinforcements, rushed off with his tiny army and a large band of native mercenaries to meet the king of the Incas.

16th century depiction of Atahualpa

Atahualpa was resting in the city of Cajamarca (in modern-day Peru), with some 80,000 troops. He had just concluded a bloody civil war with his brother Huáscar, defeating and killing him in a battle at Quipaipan. At Cajamarca, Atahualpa was preparing to march south to the Inca capital at Cuzco and assume the throne. His fighting force may not only have been exhausted but may also have been compromised by the arrival of smallpox that was sweeping south in advance of the Spanish incursion into the Inca Empire.

It seems that Atahualpa was lulled into confidence; he had allegedly been told the strangers that had recently arrived in his Empire to the north were not menacing because they were so small in number. He let the interlopers come to him and prepared for their arrival by evacuating his warriors from Cajamarca and camping on a hill nearby. When the Spanish arrived, they found an empty city. Pizarro and his troops hid in a building off the main plaza and then invited Atahualpa to come meet him. The Inca ruler, with some five or six thousand men armed with stone-age weapons like wooden clubs and obsidian bladed spears, reentered their city.

According to the story, as it was recorded later, Pizarro sent a Franciscan friar and a translator out to meet Atahualpa. The friar handed the Inca ruler a Bible and confidently informed him that he was now to submit to the authority of the Christian God. Atahualpa threw the Bible on the ground as a sign of his refusal to acknowledge the authority of the strange men and their divinity. Pizarro then sprung his ambush. His handful of armored, sword wielding and musket bearing troops rushed out into the plaza, cut down the guard of nobles surrounding Atahualpa and captured the Inca ruler.

Atahualpa Holding the Bible from an illustration in La Conquista del Peru (Seville, 1534).

Pizarro, anxious to acquire the treasure he had struggled through the South American highlands to get, demanded a ransom for Atahualpa. The Incas were ordered to bring sufficient gold to fill the captured king's cell and twice that amount in silver. The volume of treasure may have been enormous if one believes that a ransom room shown to tourists today in Cajamarca was the actual place of Atahualpa's imprisonment. The Incas complied with Pizarro's demand, but the conquistador reneged on his agreement, claiming on trumped up charges that Atahualpa had murdered his brother, practiced idolatry and attempted to revolt against the Spanish. Instead, Pizarro condemned him first to be baptized, then strangled and incinerated. This was particularly galling to the Inca, who believed that the burning of their bodies or corpses would prevent them from entering the afterlife.

Portrait depicting the death of Atahualpa, the last Sapa Inca.

Having decapitated the Inca Empire with Atahualpa's death, Pizarro then marched south on the capital of Cuzco where he resumed the butchery executing many of the Inca administrative elite. The Dominican friar Bartolomé de Las Casas (c. 1484-1566), who had first-hand experience with the actions of the Spanish conquistadors in Mexico, damned Francisco Pizarro Gonzáles for his cruelty in destroying the Empire of the Incas. In his *Short Account of the Destruction of the Indies,* of 1542, Las Casas described Pizarro's violent rampage in search of gold, writing that he "criminally murdered and plundered his way through the region, razing towns and cities to the ground and slaughtering and otherwise tormenting in the most barbaric fashion imaginable the people who lived there." As evidence of the crimes, Las Casas quoted an affidavit sworn by the Franciscan Brother Marcos de Niza, who was present at the invasion. Among many atrocities Brother Marcos wrote, "I testify that I saw with my own eyes Spaniards cutting off the hands, noses and ears of local people, both men and women, simply for the fun of it."

The destruction of trappings of Inca civilization by the Spanish was swift and in some ways quite thorough. They installed Atahualpa's brother Manco Inca Yupanqui as a puppet king, but he was not as cooperative as they had planned. He assembled a force of warriors and re-took Cuzco in 1536 but, unable to hold the city, was forced to flee into the mountains. The Spanish periodically sallied forth into the interior to engage the remaining Incas, and in 1572 captured their last stronghold and executed Túpac Amaru, who they convinced themselves was to be the last Inca king. To further the abolition of Inca culture the Spanish terminated the Inca celebration of the Inti Raymi. The cities of the Empire were destroyed, the agriculture of the Inca civilization was wrecked and the Spanish sent the Andeans to toil in the gold and silver mines where they were literally worked to death. The decimation through war and enslavement of the Inca was exacerbated by European diseases, including smallpox, typhus, influenza, diphtheria and measles.

Chapter 7: Theories about Machu Picchu

Thankfully, Machu Picchu was spared destruction at the hands of the Spanish, but the forces of decomposition are not kind to the remains of the past, and so much of what once occurred in Machu Picchu will forever remain unknown to people today. It is impossible to know for sure why Machu Picchu was built, and though it's widely believed that Machu Picchu served as a palace retreat for Pachacúti, the "Napoleon of the Andes," recently there have been alternative interpretations of both the site and the importance of Pachacúti himself.

Grand historical narratives often raise the suspicions of historians and archaeologists, and one of the most persistent of these grand narratives is that of the "Great Man." The argument is that history has been shaped by certain individuals, implying that without their existence, none of the events they were involved with would have happened. In contrast to this is the school of Processual Archaeology. In general, archaeologists rarely know anything about the individuals who lived in the places they excavate and instead look at broad social trends and transformations. The Processualists take this even a step further by focusing upon the study of trends ("processes") and seeing long-term change as the most significant element in human history.

The elegance of the story that links Pachacúti with the conquest of the Andes and the creation of perhaps the most spectacular architectural site in the history of South America has an internal coherency and an appeal, especially for those who admire the ancient Inca. However, Processual archaeologists have recently begun to examine the structural circumstances in Incan society that facilitated Pachacúti's conquests: the organization of the military, administration, lines of communication, and especially agriculture. These studies have concluded that the Urubamba River Valley and the other rich agricultural lands around Cuzco form the foundation for the empire as much as Pachacúti's conquest.[30]

Further work has been done in the re-interpretation of Machu Picchu itself. These studies examine the evidence (or lack thereof) for the complex being a palace and instead find that it has far more similarities with other holy pilgrimage sites, especially the Island of the Sun in Lake Titicaca to the south. By examining the layout of the structure, as well as the alignments of various buildings with both the landscape and astronomical phenomena, some scholars argue that Machu Picchu is not a palace but a holy place which may not even date to the reign of Pachacúti.[31] This analysis fits well with the interpretation of Incan history that places the Urubamba Valley at the center of the Incan ability to construct their empire. In the end, it is impossible to know if this interpretation is correct or

---

30 "A Processual Study of Inka State Formation" by R. Alan Covey in the *Journal of Anthropological Archaeology* (2002) no 22 pp 333-357; *How the Incas Built Their Heartland* by R. Alan Covey (2007).
31 "At the Other End of the Sun's Path: A New Interpretation of Machu Picchu" (2010) by Giulio Magli in the *Nexus Network Journal* V 12, No 2, pp 321-341

not, but the strength of the evidence ensures that the theory demands mention in any serious conversation about the history of the site.

The general public is particularly fascinated with ancient ruins that have an air of mystery about them, and there are many mysteries surrounding Machu Picchu, including why it was created and who ordered its construction. However, perhaps the greatest and longest-lasting mystery has been the question of why it was abandoned. The builders went to incredible lengths to construct it, level the mountain, re-route waterways, and literally reshape the topography itself. Given the fact that the Spanish did not conquer or deface Machu Picchu, it's astonishing that the site was completely abandoned only about 100 years after it was created.

Scholars may never be able to determine exactly why Machu Picchu was left to the jungle, but it is possible to rule out a number of scenarios. For example, Machu Picchu was definitely not destroyed by the Spanish conquistadores; in fact, there is no mention or record amongst the early Spanish chroniclers of Machu Picchu, and there's no way that a site of this size and importance would have been overlooked in their records. Moreover, there are no traces of destruction in the archaeological record: no burned buildings, no out-of-place human remains, no signs of struggle. Perhaps most notably, the religious sites of Machu Picchu were not desecrated, including the Intihuatana. At other Incan ruins, the Catholic priests who accompanied the Spanish zealously went out of their way to destroy all of the Intihuatana they could find, and they were remarkably effective at scrubbing the indigenous religion and mythology from existence. The Spanish knew these sites were the heart of the Incan sun religion, which itself was a justification for the reign of the Inca emperors, making it essential for the Spanish to destroy them while claiming the land. However, the Intihuatana at Machu Picchu is remarkably well-preserved.

Another common misconception is that Machu Picchu was abandoned because it was so geographically isolated and was thus uneconomical to maintain. This theory is based more on the nature of the Sacred Valley around the site today, because the region is largely depopulated, covered in verdant forest and quite difficult to reach by normal forms of transportation. However, as noted before, in the 15th and 16th centuries, this was one of the richest agricultural regions of the empire and was a source of great power and wealth for the Inca. Moreover, this importance continued until the last days of the empire's power. The sites of Vitcos, Vilcabamba and Choquequirao were all located further along the Anti Suyu road from Cuzco and were among the very last strongholds of independent Incan government, despite their relative isolation. It is therefore possible to eliminate the argument that Machu Picchu was simply too far away from the centers of power to justify the continued expense of operating it.

What are the remaining theories to explain the abandonment of Machu Picchu? A number of possibilities have been proposed. One of the more plausible is that the native population was devastated by the smallpox epidemic of 1527, a disease inadvertently brought to the New World by the Spanish. As indigenous groups across the New World soon discovered to their horror, foreign diseases were perhaps the most effective weapon at the Europeans' disposal. The Inca were actually devastated by the illness even before the Conquistadores had arrived.[32] It is estimated that smallpox may have killed two-thirds of the population (including the emperor), which would have also destroyed the mit'a system of labor. Without the mit'a, roads and trails would have quickly fallen into disrepair.[33] However, there is still no evidence to suggest a smallpox epidemic hit Machu Picchu; recent investigation of the 74 bodies found at the site did not indicate the presence of the disease.[34]

In the end, the ultimate fate of Machu Picchu remains a mystery, but what is known is that the site was no longer occupied by the time the Spanish arrived. Its existence remained part of local folklore for centuries afterwards, but there were no known attempts to explore or document it until the early 20th century.

Chapter 8: Modern Machu Picchu

After the collapse of both the Incan Empire and the colonial Spanish empire, it took the rise of a new power in the hemisphere for attention to once again be turned to Machu Picchu. The "Discoverer" of Machu Picchu was a U.S. citizen named Hiram Bingham III, who in many ways embodied the late 19th and early 20th century imperial spirit in North America. The Bingham's descend from an old line of New England families with a multi-generational connection to Yale University, and his grandfather, Hiram Bingham I, was the leader of the first group of Protestant missionaries to the Kingdom of Hawaii,[35] and his son (Hiram Jr.) followed his footsteps. Born in Honolulu, Hiram Jr. was educated in Connecticut (including Yale) and became a Pacific Island missionary.[36]

---

32 *Guns, Germs and Steel* (1997) by Jared Diamond. W.W. Norton Publishers.
33 "Machu Picchu Abandoned: How they kept it secret" by Gary Ziegler. Accessed online at: http://www.adventurespecialists.org/mpabandoned.html
34 "Diet, Residential Origin, and Pathology at Machu Picchu, Peru" (2012) by Bethany L. Turner and George J. Armelagos. In *American Journal of Physical Anthropology* 149:71-83
35 "Bingham, Hiram, 1789-1869, American Congregationalist missionary." (2013). In *The Columbia Encyclopedia*. Retrieved from http://www.credoreference.com.libezproxy2.syr.edu/entry/columency/bingham_hiram_1789_1869_american_congregationalist_missionary
36 "Bingham, Hiram, 1831-1908, American Congregationalist missionary." (2013). In *The Columbia Encyclopedia*. Retrieved from http://www.credoreference.com.libezproxy2.syr.edu/entry/columency/bingham_hiram_1831_1908_american_congregationalist_missionary

Hiram Bingham III

The third Hiram Bingham, the one whose fate became intertwined with that of Machu Picchu, was born in Honolulu in 1875. He was educated first in Honolulu and then in New England before attending Yale University, where he attained his BA in 1898, the same year the United States annexed Hawaii. He went on to get his doctorate from Harvard and then began to teach history, first in Harvard, then Princeton (under Woodrow Wilson's administration of the University) and finally in Yale in 1907, where he taught South American history.[37]

It was on a trip in 1908 to the First Pan-American Scientific Congress in Chile that Bingham's interest in Incan archaeology was piqued. He visited Peru on the way home and traveled to the ruined Incan citadel of Choquequirao, where he became further entranced by the concept of lost cities. In 1911, he returned, this time accompanied by the Yale Expedition to Peru, and he would return again in 1912 and 1915 on trips that were partially funded by the National Geographic Society and Yale.

Of course, those subsequent trips were financed almost wholly because of his 1911 trip, during which

---

37 "Bingham, Hiram, 1875-1956, American archaeologist, historian, and statesman." (2013). In *The Columbia Encyclopedia*. Retrieved from http://www.credoreference.com.libezproxy2.syr.edu/entry/columency/bingham_hiram_1875_1956_american_archaeologist_historian_and_statesman

he was led to Machu Picchu by a local guide. While Bingham was more than willing to claim this as his "discovery," it was known to locals and was apparently visited by several other Europeans before his arrival. What set Bingham apart, however, were his connections to two powerful American institutions: Yale University and the National Geographic Society. Together with a public fascination about "lost cities," especially since the 1885 publication of *King Solomon's Mines*, these institutions and Bingham captivated a global audience with the tales and images of Machu Picchu, the "Lost City of the Inca." Yale and the National Geographic Society also found a convenient figure in Bingham. Dashingly handsome in an age where photography became more commonplace, he was the American answer to great British explorers like Livingstone and Stanley. It was also helpful that Bingham's adventures sold numerous copies of the *National Geographic Magazine*, not to mention the fact he brought thousands of objects (upwards of 40,000 by some estimates) back to Yale and its Peabody Museum. The objects became a feature of the new museum building opened in 1925.[38]

A picture of Machu Picchu in 1911

Even though Bingham is still credited for the discovery, in recent years a number of rivals to the status of "first outsider" have emerged. Peruvian records show that in the 1860s, a German named Augusto Berns built a sawmill nearby and obtained official permission to loot the site. There is even evidence that Bingham had access to Berns' notes in his search for Incan sites, and the sawmill appears on an 1875 map of the area. Even in Bingham's day, a British Protestant missionary named Thomas

---

38 "In the Wonderland of Peru" (1913) by Hiram Bingham in *National Geographic Magazine*. Accessed online at: http://ngm.nationalgeographic.com/1913/04/machu-picchu/bingham-text

Payne and a German engineer named J.M. von Hassel both plausibly claimed to have visited the location first.[39] To an extent, however, it doesn't matter whether Bingham was the "first" or not, because it is undeniable that his presence at Machu Picchu forever transformed the site from a half-hidden, half-forgotten ruin to a "lost city" of mystery and beauty. There is no dispute that Bingham's journey focused the world's attention on the Urubamba Valley.

When Bingham first arrived at Machu Picchu, the ancient Incan roads to the site were long-lost, forcing him and his guides to cut their way through the thick forest and scale the mountains by hand for six days. Things have become considerably easier for the modern visitor, however. Many visitors start in the ancient capital of Cuzco and take the luxurious PeruRail train from the city to the ruins. The more adventurous tourists can use the modern "Inca Trail," a footpath that starts in southern Colombia and ends in northern Chile, following the ancient Incan roads. In many areas, the Trail is still in its original form, with stones paved by the laborers of the Incan Empire.

If anything, Machu Picchu is most threatened today by the presence of too many visitors. In the 1950s and 60s, there was only one guard on the site who gave private tours to anyone who made it up there, but after the end of the Peruvian guerrilla conflict in the 1990s and shrewd tourism marketing by Peru, visitors began flocking to the site. PeruRail opened direct links to Cuzco in 1999. While this was a boon for modern tourists, it also meant that the site was increasingly encroached upon, and the fragile state of many of the ruins was under threat. Machu Picchu was generating $40 million a year in tourism income for Peru, but in 2000, UNESCO put the site on their official endangered list, and the Peruvian government and the United Nations Education, Scientific and Cultural Organization (UNESCO) worked together to limit the number of visitors to 2,500 a day.[40]

Not surprisingly, Machu Picchu has become far more than simply a place for international tourists and their currency. Over the past few decades, it has emerged as the preeminent national symbol for Peruvians. In 1983, the Peruvians submitted Machu Picchu to UNESCO's list of "World Heritage Sites." This designation exists for the world's most exceptional places, including cultural products like the Statue of Liberty, natural wonders like Mount Kenya, and even some fusion of the two, like Machu Picchu.[41] Since that time, Machu Picchu has further skyrocketed in local esteem, as evidenced by the nation's participation in the New7Wonders of the World competition in 2007. The New7Wonders project was an attempt to create a new list of the "Seven Wonders of the World" through a combination of expert panels and online voting. A number of nations rallied their citizenry to participate in the vote and get their national sites into the official list, especially in Latin America, where nationalism was stoked to get votes. This focus helped bring victory to Chichen Itza in Mexico, Christ the Redeemer in Rio de Janeiro, and Machu Picchu.[42]

---

39 "So, was the Lost City of Machu Picchu ever lost?" by Leonard Doyle, in *The Independent*, Nov 8 2008, accessed online at: http://www.independent.co.uk/news/world/americas/so-was-the-lost-city-of-machu-picchu-ever-lost-1058004.html; "The Fights of Machu Picchu: Who Got There First?" by Simon Romero in *The New York Times* Nov 8 2008, accessed online at: http://www.nytimes.com/2008/12/08/world/americas/08iht-journal.1.18479442.html?_r=0
40 "Saving Machu Picchu" by Whitney Dangerfield in *The Smithsonian Magazine* 1 May 2007. Accessed online at: http://www.smithsonianmag.com/people-places/machu.html?c=y&page=1
41 "Historic Sanctuary of Machu Picchu" at the UNESCO World Heritage Homepage http://whc.unesco.org/en/list/274
42 http://world.new7wonders.com/

Peruvian pride in their "Lost City" led their Antarctic expedition to name the nation's only permanent base in the southern continent the "Machu Picchu Base," a summer-only facility constructed in 1989 that holds up to 32 researchers.[43] And perhaps most fittingly, Machu Picchu has lent its name to an object in outer space. Discovered in 1991, asteroid 8277 Machu-Picchu is a relatively small body floating in the main Asteroid Belt. It was found by researchers in the European Southern Observatory, a massive astronomical facility located in the deserts of northern Chile - once a part of Incan territory.[44]

Machu Picchu has also entered national and international politics. UNESCO's classification of the site as endangered was a major embarrassment for the Peruvian government, which has since sought to improve its control of the site. Furthermore, there was a dispute around 2005 over the illegal construction by a local mayor of an automobile bridge connecting the site to the road network. The site gained even further political currency around 2008 when the Peruvian government began to prepare for the 100th anniversary of Bingham's first expedition to the site. They began to insist that the artifacts Bingham removed from the area, which included thousands of objects and mummified remains, be returned from Yale University to Peru. After a very public and at times nasty exchange, Yale returned the objects in early 2012, a major victory for the Peruvian administration.[45] Today, Yale and a Peruvian university, San Antonio Abad University are constructing a facility for the display and study of these items in Cuzco. San Antonio Abad is itself a colonial-era institution, having been founded in 1692.

The future of Machu Picchu is far from settled. More and more visitors seek every year to visit the site and are coming now via car, bus, train and even helicopter. These increase the preservation challenges for the hard-pressed Peruvian government, which relies on the income generated by the famous site. Peru must strike a balance between allowing visitors to make money while also protecting the site's future. That said, the site's popularity inside Peru and its role as a symbol of Peruvian national pride and history should ensure financial backing for preservation efforts well into the future.

---

43 "COMNAP: Instituto Antartico Peruano (INANPE)", accessed online at
https://www.comnap.aq/Members/INANPE/SitePages/Home.aspx
44 Asteroid data available at: http://ssd.jpl.nasa.gov/sbdb.cgi?sstr=8277
45 "Finders Not Keepers: Yale Returns Artifacts to Peru" by Diane Orson, published by NPR News 18 Dec 2011. Accessed online at:
http://www.npr.org/2012/01/01/143653050/finders-not-keepers-yale-returns-artifacts-to-peru